The lion is a large cat of the genus
Panthera native to Africa and India
Length: 1.8 - 2.1 m (Male, Head and
body), 1.6 - 1.8 m (Female, Head and
body)

Tigers are huge, strong, fanged predators that eat dozens of pounds of meat per day and need acres of expensive high-security enclosures

Common Names: Panther, Black panther, black leopard, black jaguar
Habitat: Forests, swamplands, grasslands
Location: Asia, America, Africa
Life Span: 12-15 years

Foxes are more like cats than dogs. Similar to cats, foxes are nocturnal. Foxes live in underground dens. .Foxes are smelly. Foxes make 40 different sounds.

Crocodiles can survive for a long time without food.

Elephants are the largest existing land animals. Elephants are big vegetarians. In the wild, they eat a wide variety of plants, from savannah grasses, shrubs, and herbs, to woody trees, bark, and fruits.

monkeys can use their hands and feet for holding on to branches. Monkeys are found in two main regions of the world, so scientists have grouped them as either Old World monkeys or New World monkeys.

Zebra Stripes Are Most Likely a Form of Pest Control. There Are 3 Species of Zebra in the Wild.
Each Species Has Different Types of Stripes. They Are Impressive Climbers

Bears are mammals that belong to the family Ursidae. They can be as small as four feet long and about 60 pounds (the sun bear) to as big as eight feet long

The Inland Taipan or famously known as 'fierce snake', has the most toxic venom in the world. It can yield as much as 110mg in one bite, which is enough to kill around 100 people or over 2.5 lakh mice.

the most universally recommended scorpion species to keep as a pet is the emperor scorpion. Scorpions are also not usually aggressive creatures, but rather wary, timid, and retiring.

There are 5 species of rhino in the world. Rhinos can weigh over 3 tones. Black and white rhinos are both, in fact, grey. They're called bulls and cows. Rhinos have poor vision.

Wolves have 42 teeth.
They have four toes with claws in an oval
shape. Wolves mate for life. A litter of
wolves is usually 4 to 6 pups. Wolves can
run at 36 to 38 MPH

goose, any of various large heavy-bodied waterfowl intermediate in size and build between large ducks and swans. A female goose is called a dame

There are 360+ hummingbird species.
Hummingbirds are incredibly tuned in.
Hummingbirds visit hundreds of flowers
each day.

Kingfishers feed on a wide variety of prey. They are most famous for hunting and eating fish, frog and others amphibians, annelid worms, molluscs, insects, spiders, centipedes, reptiles

Seals Are Part of the Pinniped Order of Marine Mammals. Seals Prefer Cold Sea Waters. Seal Species Come in Different Sizes. Seals Are Related to Bears, Skunks, and Badgers. The Largest Seal Weighs More Than Four Tons

They have a big appetite.
They mate for life.
Male seahorses have babies!
Their tails are a valuable tool.
Speaking of predators, they
don't have all that many.